DAVID MILLER
FOR ALL THAT'S LOST

Newton-le-Willows

Published in the United Kingdom in 2025
by The Knives Forks And Spoons Press,
51 Pipit Avenue,
Newton-le-Willows,
Merseyside,
WA12 9RG.

ISBN 978-1-916590-12-0

Copyright © David Miller 2025.

The right of David Miller to be identified as the author of this work has been asserted by them in accordance with the Copyrights, Designs and Patents Act of 1988. All rights reserved. No part of this publication may be reproduced, stored in a retrieval system, transmitted in any form or by any means, electronic, photocopying, recording or otherwise, without prior permission of the publisher.

Acknowledgments:

'Nowhere' was written in 1972 and revised in 1974. It was published in the Australian literary journal *Etymspheres*, series 2/1, Marysville, Victoria, [1974], as 'OU-TOPOS'. It was then very slighted revised before being published as a limited edition broadsheet from Kater Murr's Press in 2025.

'Out-takes' was written circa 2022 and was published in the online journal *otoliths*.

'The Remains', 'Cenotaph' and 'For All That's Now Lost' were written in 2024. 'The Remains' has appeared in *ETC*. The others appear here for the first time.

'Again: Black Ink in the Palace of the Bees' appeared from Kater Murr's Press in 2024. God bless the Cat.

Cover image: ink painting by David Miller, copyright © David Miller 2025.

FOR ALL THAT'S LOST

Contents

The Remains   7

Cenotaph   11

For All That's Now Lost   15

Again: Black Ink in the Palace of the Bees   39

Nowhere (Ou-topos)   45

Out-takes   49

Notes   63

The Remains

For All That's Lost

If
the building,

winding and stacked,
was destroyed

by fire –

if we
destroyed it –

there might be evidence
left –

archival –
All the things

I'd worked on
and left behind –

If trapped
then now released

with any luck.
She was walking alongside me

on Charing Cross Road –
"I know you're not really here,"

David Miller

I said,

"but please tell me if you'll come back to me."

The ethical is prior to ontology –

What surpasses death

is transgressive,

not violence.

Cenotaph

A nightjar calls.

My brush makes a circle
in ink

freehand and thus
unlike your precise

stone
building.

Light – the sun? –

circles
the cypresses.

In the night,
stars

push me to my limits.

For All That's Now Lost

The blackbird in the garden
hops beside me

and opens his yellow beak
as if he might begin speaking.

He flew by my window
or else my window flew by him –

said so often,
it's now hand to mouth, mouth to hand.

David Miller

Little bird,
little bird –

he has already spoken
and continues to speak.

A hand on which a bird rests and sings
is the hand for me.

Hand to hand,
mouth to mouth.

A shadow kissed.

David Miller

Cut thumb. Orange
ink. My

walking stick
blacks out.

For All That's Lost

Kissed

by a shadow

but not even a leaf

knew.

David Miller

Chin-chucked
by a notorious gangster

because she was smoking
a large cigar –

my wife laughed to recall.

On the station platform,
on the underground train –

what was said, what was shared.
Station signs unreadable.

Where to alight?
Where? Fate, illegible.

For All That's Lost

A chance
that's blind,

deaf and dumb.
Orange ink

supposedly red –
not gold, at any rate,

as I'd hoped. No
lead for alchemy,

either.

David Miller

Lead not stacked,
not splashed against a wall,

not dropped and
caught or not

in a hand – and this filmed –

For All That's Lost

Does a spirit
bleed?

My walking stick
blacks out.

David Miller

A bush with a bird
is the bush for me.

You flew by my window.
Not even a leaf knew.

Yet a bush with a bird
is a shadow kissed. My

walking stick
blacks out. A shadow

that's kissed
is the shadow.

Male,
female.

They gave me whiskey and salted peanuts – "Please, drink, we do not drink, but you drink," the wife said. I was utterly unused to whiskey, but of course I drank.

Fragmented images *building* a narrative rather than merely interrupting or illustrating it.

Fragmented images *building* a narrative rather than merely interrupting or illustrating it.

Dispersed narrative.

Unfolding, regenerating narrative.

Stones upon stones

that had once

been botanicals.

A stone wall

yet not

a stone wall?

A wall of winds,

bushes and grasses.

David Miller

Stones upon stones.

A cat

walks along the stone wall,

meows as it nears.

Otherwise, silence.

Winds amongst trees,
bushes and grasses.

My friend plays a zither
long in his family

and for long unplayed.

My clarinet
speaks and sings.

David Miller

Fragmented images *building* a narrative rather than merely interrupting or illustrating it.

Go back to the *Gospels* and *Acts*.

For All That's Lost

Shadows arch,
arch and cry

under arches,
dark waters surging.

David Miller

Blood that disappears.
In the glass

you died, and
I died. Blood

disappears
and reappears.

For All That's Lost

Outside in the garden in rain

a

squirrel had climbed
to the studio roof

having first scaled
the adjacent trees. It then

climbed down the

same way. Stones
upon stones. The

blackbird turns
his bright eye

towards me and opens
his yellow beak. The glass –

I can no longer think of death
without thinking of your dying.

David Miller

Go back to the *Gospels* and *Acts*.

Glass:
white, green, brown, crimson,

blue. And black –
even black –

even without
traceries of lead.

A tree. An angel.
A nativity. A cruc-

ifixion. A
resurrection.

Thinking back to that winter, many years ago, when I was in Paris and drank whiskey at the home of a Japanese artist. He took me to his studio and showed me his paintings, which were stacked around the walls; he spoke no English, his wife spoke a little, I spoke neither French nor Japanese, so there was little conversation. But I'll always remember their hospitality, even inviting me to visit again (which I didn't, due to sudden illness). The paintings were bold yet also in some way humble, if that makes sense, and almost heraldic or emblematic, however abstract the paintings, in their simplicity and directness. I thought of them as having a Zen-like stillness and silence; later I read about how he and his wife liked fast cars, and that he was inspired by the instant communication of road signs when travelling at high speeds: was this completely contradictory? I'd like to believe not.

David Miller

The isles of the dead. *Peripli*
are disputed

when not denied. Black
waters and black sky.

Black is everything that black can be.
Lights across the bridge –

lights spiralling
in the darkness –

and I am not the one at the wheel.

(In memory of Dodo, with love)

Again: Black Ink in the Palace of the Bees

For All That's Lost

David Miller

For All That's Lost

David Miller

Nowhere
(Ou-topos)

Seasons. Distress. For all we know I may, I may be back: days, months, year. Again. For all we. Scream at her: at the clouds, the water; shout. The stones, she said, stones, the stones, said, they'll – together, not, together further. Float. Easily.

Durations. Said: what: birds ascending the sky. What she. Birds. Birds. Birds. Birds. Gliding. Without meaning. Gliding. Meaning.

Adamantine. Glare. Light. Fool. She said nothing. I turned. I turned. Looking forever.

Why? She said nothing. Nothing. I. Why? Always.

Abruptly. The soft. Continuance. Intently. She said: across the mouth. Be quiet for a while. Be quiet.

You're so. Anyone as bad as you before, so nervous, so anxious. What are you afraid of? As. Knot.

Turned my head. Saying: she didn't come. As negative, she said. Who are you? Who, really, is – ? The Law? Is? The *Dao?* Is? Christ? She said? Who? What? I am?

You're the most nervous, frightened. Again. She. With. A little. I don't. I don't. To see you this way. To help. To be. Your friend. Your friend.

To look straight at her. To hell.

She lit a cigarette. Why? she said. To see me?

Yes.

Raised only by the clear, the semi-bright, the transparent colouring. Ordinary things.

Fixed. Adamantine. Eyes. She knew that. Knew. Knew. Surely she did.

She said. As. Half-exasperated. Half. Half-mocking. Oh. Oh. Oh do. I'd be interested – the secrets, the rain, the filth, stuffed, the common things, *ghastly, ghastly,* but – Oh, oh!

From a cold distance. Continuance. Is it – ? Hand. Is it – ? Is it good?

PLEASE. Said: Where should I – ? For Chrissake, I said. The cruelty. I can't, I can't, I can't, I can't.

To make out it *is* a pure love. Hopeless. Tragic? To make that out. Not to see. To stare: with cruelty and good intent. Beauty.

Did you think? To help you? Help you to learn? Hoping I'd? Confused. Oh you. You. – is good?

Quiet and harsh: is supernatural. Of necessity. Of. Good.

She said:

If you don't know why. Came. To see. If you don't know why, say. That. To see me. Why. Speak.

Nothingness. A little. To look into. At the side. At the side. Of her head. Of her head. A gap. Between. The durations, staring. Soft. Continuance.

Was always the way, before, terribly, to *get out*.

– Perhaps you'd prefer. Perhaps you'd prefer me – to leave? Stood up. The table. Doesn't always, I said, why, hurriedly, there may be. Again. She seated herself. I don't know. Know. What to do.

Clouds. To see into. Intermediaries. To soften. A little. The hills. A little. Colours drifting and floating across the walls. To look at her. She. To look at me. So terribly beautiful, so terribly gentle, the one, terribly loving, close, from her chair. Do you – ? To be afraid? In time? Time? To defend an illusion? To defend a self? To defend a self, a self which is an illusion?

Cut him! I said. The blood, ordinary.

The café opened, to the wind. To see. Again. Shouted. Stood. Stepped away.

(For Elizabeth Gaskin)

Out-takes

For All That's Lost

1.

implied:
an eye

at a

dismemberment
of a woman

in lamplight
a lamp

she still holds

shown:
the bachelors

shown:
the bride

shown:
the chocolate mill

(sperm)

David Miller

elsewhere shown:

(by others)

the razor across the eye

or an eye

peeps

through the hole

not content

with the urinal

or the bottle-rack

or

the Mona Lisa

with moustache

& caption

& yet the retinal

denigrated

David Miller

or else Robert Smithson

's

spiral

jetty

as

an alternative

2.

did Duchamp
ever discard

discs of ice
from bird baths?

did Gertrude Stein
ever talk to the mechanics

who fixed her car
while she wrote

regardless
of the noise?

David Miller

the ego is always there

in everything

except when it isn't

Picasso was leading the way
while others were following

& Americans
were being made

or one American

3.

Jesus of Nazareth
raised the dead

Apollonius of Tyana
raised the dead

– a climate of miracles

4.

rescued
from a diving suit ...

with a silly
moustache

outlandish
at least

& much money ...

he'd found his way
through painted landscapes

of burning giraffes
& melting watches

& Mae West's lips
as a sofa

to Hollywood
&

David Miller

to Andy Warhol's

glamour

factory

& Jesus of Nazareth

suspended in space

without nails

& a woman's eye

still slit

5.

poetry isn't painting

poetry isn't music

nor is painting poetry

nor is it music

nor music

poetry or painting

nor is poetry ... is it

anthropology?

no nor religion

yet each might learn

from each other

possibly

in some instances

but not become the other

David Miller

Gertrude following Pablo

writing following painting

& protected by the Vichy government

nothing seemed to ruffle her

huge & haughty

& self-content

in her genius

snow blind

(for John Levy)

Notes:

Although the sequence 'All That's Now Lost' is mostly in free verse, with a few prose interludes or "interruptions", and 'Nowhere' is a prose poem, and although they were written decades apart, there are connections, just the same. They are both about loss, the one about what never came to any fruition and the other one about what did. They both explore techniques that have concerned me at various times throughout my writing life, including repetition, variation and permutation along with fragmentation and juxtaposition. These concerns are evident in *South London Mix*, for example, which was written in 1973 and published a couple of years later by the prestigious Gaberbocchus Press. I have mostly used these techniques quite freely, but I've never felt the slightest need to apologise for this.

The notorious gangster referred to in 'All That's Now Lost' was one of the Kray twins, most likely (although not necessarily) Reggie Kray. My late wife Dodo would indeed laugh about this incident, although she also admitted she was terrified of the Krays – as well she probably should have been. (This entire note is of course purely anecdotal.)

Black is everything… is a paraphrase from something that the poet Robert Lax wrote to me many years ago.

'Nowhere' was influenced by Expressionist plays, those of August Stramm and Oscar Kokoschka in particular.

DM, August 2024

David Miller was born in Melbourne, Australia, but has lived in the UK for many years. His more recent publications include *Spiritual Letters* (Contraband Books, 2017 / Spuyten Duyvil, 2022), *Towards a Menagerie* (Chax Press, 2019), *Matrix (1-2)* (Guillemot Press, 2020 / Spuyten Duyvil, 2024), *Afterword* (Shearsman Books, 2022), *circle square triangle* (Spuyten Duyvil, 2022), *Some Other Shadows* (Knives Forks and Spoons Press, 2022), *Time, Wisdom and Koalas* (Chax Press, 2023), *(close)* (KFS Press, 2023) and *What Is and Might Be and Then Otherwise* (KFS, 2024). He is also a painter and a musician.

www.ingramcontent.com/pod-product-compliance
Lightning Source LLC
Chambersburg PA
CBHW041524090426
42737CB00038B/113